Mystery and Imperfection

Mystery and Imperfection

Poems by

T.P. Bird

Cover design by Shay Culligan
Cover image by Ashkan Forouzani on Unsplash

ISBN: 978-1-63980-027-8

Kelsay Books
502 South 1040 East, A-119
American Fork, Utah 84003
Kelsaybooks.com

Acknowledgments

BoomerLit: "The Interview"

Common Ground Review: "Visit to a Country Graveyard"

Miller's Pond: "Autumn Song," "Canoeing on Sunfish Pond," "Evening Song on Saylor Road"

Penwood Review: "Earth, Wind, Water and Fire"

Poetry Quarterly: "Some Thoughts in Early Winter"

Relief Quarterly: "A Short History of Failure"

Tiny Seed Literary Journal: "Auger Falls"

Contents

Mystery

Upon Finding the Lost Haystack of Claude Monet

Wandering an upstate meadow
and finding a farmer's hay-*roll,*
I knew instantly Claude Monet
would have painted it, even
though its colors were in
shades of brown and streaks of
black and amber. No lavenders,
pinks, and reds as seen through
Claude Monet's ingenious eye.

We know Monet dealt only with
genuine French haystacks.
As any Francophile will tell you,
his models were cut from very
special *Gallic* grass—growing
not only in artless green, but in
all the colors of a French artist's
pallet. And, French *soleil* & *plein
air* produce an amazing spread of
hues. Just think what that Dutch
painter saw under the *Provence* sun.

Yet, I believe Claude Monet would
have found my upstate hay-roll
a truly aesthetic delight—for I am
certain he would perceive within it,
more colors than I *ever* could.

Adam and the Dance

The Lord God said,
"It is not good for the man to be alone"
—Genesis 2:18

Hearing the wind play silly
tunes through my body, I
realize: I'm missing a rib!

If I am to be awkward like
this, the music must stop
while I look for an answer.

Surprising me, my rib sits
in a chair across from me,
now a vessel for pulse and

breath, much like myself—
yet...different. Reaching,
curious to touch, I brace my

fall against her fragile frame.
And in the smoothest motion,
this rib and I begin to move

together in a most natural
rhythm.

At the Allergist

Lives in these rooms
this afternoon are being
measured in ten minute
intervals—the attention
span of postmodern man.
It's every six hundred
seconds—back and forth
with a clip-board in hand,
listening for the egg timer
to ding, waiting for any
rejoinder from
the alien substance
injected just under
the skin.

Ah, mold has caused
little bongos on a
neighbor's arm;
dirty little scoundrels!

Killing time between jabs,
I'm trying to understand
the print on the wall
just above my head.
A nude woman, viewed
from the rear, is set
against a checkerboard
pattern. A Christ-like
figure hangs in midair
in the distance, while
Abraham Lincoln
occupies a square
at the bottom right.
Most likely the scene

of an allergic reaction
that no doubt, caught
the attention of patient
and doctors alike.

Observation on a Noonday Stroll

Light drizzle,
a shadowless day.
A stretch of shiny rails,
rain blackened ties
laced with bursts
of thick, orange
leaves.

A middle-aged blonde
woman in low-heeled,
dressy black shoes
walks on a cinder path
beside the tracks.
She wears
a purple dress,
long, lightweight coat—
unbuttoned and free
on her shoulders.

Her left hand holds
aloft a large black &
white umbrella.
An extended right hand
holds a short lease—
pulled taut by the
weight of a large
brown dog.

Beside the woman
walks a black cat,
keeping pace in
perfect time with
the others.

It's like a scene
in a Broadway play
and I expect to hear
music at any moment.

Visit to a Country Graveyard

Their first names are emblems
of the era: Philander, Chauncey,
Cornelius, Alonzo among the men.
Polly, Bela, Lydia and Alice Mae—
some of the women who joined
their husbands in death in mid
19th Century rural America.

Old Country Rule Number One:
Never put a graveyard on tillable
land. A plateau-like hill as this
was perfect for burying the dead—
being already lifted part way to
heaven on a rise of high ground
above the road to a nearby village.

Strangely at ease in this old grave
yard among tall trees, I feel Mary
Matilda, wife of Ephram, would
welcome me sitting on her stone.
From here, I begin to imagine
unsung lives—names and dates on
lichened stones set in the earth of
this shady place.

With great certainty, Hannah
Abraham's stone has hand and
finger pointed toward the sky—
though after many years, it now
stops at a canopy of ancient maples.
If not acquainted with religious
symbols, one might think her a
first prize winner at the county fair.

Old Fred Johnson, born in 1880,
buried his wife Alice Mae in 1910,
but never got around to dying.
Today his headstone remains
noticeably unmarked. Perhaps,
Fred's poor progeny didn't want
to invest money in such an
unprofitable matter as the date
of dad's death.

Folks named Osborne are buried
under small markers—off by
themselves on the lonely north
slope. One can suppose they never
got along with their neighbors,
and chose to remain unsociable
throughout all eternity.

Arraying the grave of Bela Sanford—
died 1876 at 67 years—a detailed
cast iron monument complete with
spire, drapes, roses, and four cast
panels: clasped hands, a reef of
flowers, a vine covered cross and
lilies of the valley. Upon the spire
I ascertain an ear of corn, an hour
glass with scythe, and an anchor
to hold life down in a windy storm.
Oh, these 19th Century symbols of
faith—aiding a soul to accept death
as an event of distinction—an idea
foreign to *au courant* Americans as
a life on the dark side of the moon.

Meditation

It's said, animals don't experience
time. If so, Eleanor, the adopted
cat, is ignorant of minutes passing
us by as we watch from inside a
snow squall, which leaves barely
a trace—this despite the fury
it seemed.

It's also said the human creature
is seized and held by time because
we anticipate hardship, loss and
death. Yes, other times and other
snows have fallen hard—burying
my joy deep.

Yet what choice do we have but to
live as the bulb lives: in the shelter
of the earth. In some spring I will rise.
These thoughts wrap around my mind
as my hands now wrap around a cold
mug of once hot tea, while all my
accumulated days lay around me
like a winter not yet ended.

Evening Song on Saylor Road

Perhaps it's near the end of history;
once more evening falls slowly,
        almost imperceptibly,
over the mid-summer meadow.

A condensing mist settles silently
into the more low-lying landscape,
and soon drifts across the dirt road
like a community of ghost-farmers
leaving behind the memory
        of ancient hay—scythed,
raked and packed in empty wagons.

Meadow birds issue their last song
before nightfall—the sound of
dripping water: *ker-plunk, ker-plunk.*
Ballooning frogs in a nearby pond
broadcast their ancient language—
declaiming a severe mercy once
misunderstood by Egyptians of old.

The trees that trim the meadow are
a dark emerald, but quickly turn into
black silhouettes as the light fades
in the west.

It won't be long: the bob-o-links
will say goodnight to each other and
fall asleep in the deep, dark grass—
unaware that the reaper comes soon.

Autumn Song

Evenings are taking on that quality known as
      crisp; three lone birds

silhouetted against the darkening sky almost
      cause the air to crackle

at the moving of their wings. Once emerald
      cornfields are turning with age

to an afterglow of tan and gold; soon the
      farmers will cut them down,

and the ground will fall asleep, like it has
      for many generations,

for the earth is on the verge of rest from
      a season of toiling and growing.

While sitting on the back porch searching
      the sky for signs of change, the

groundhog sits on the edge of his hole looking
      forward to the winter

dreams of hibernation. Not having left, many
      birds are checking wind and

light for signals like magnets that pull from
      the south; yet, many will remain

with brooding shoulders within bare trees,
      keeping the silence within

their tiny, fragile bones. Poets go inward as
        the days grow short;

in the cold winter nights we will listen for the
        faint ring of colliding stars;

myths once hidden in dense summer growth
        become visible in the

sharp, clean air. The huntsman will enter the
        wood, his eyes full of

searching, his hands full of feverish hope.
        There is no anger nor

malice here—only the annual return of blood
        to the skull of the hunter.

Soon the hills will light up in a fury of color—
        the once stable green leaves

gone crazy in the lunacy of old age. The moon
        itself will become full of

expectation at watching the rabbits run wild
        across winter's snowy fields,

leaving behind a clear trail that spring will not
        remember. The owls will

hold court, flying from the woods to their
        judicial benches at the edge of fields—

to pronounce their nature's judgment upon
  the creatures who live close

to that terrible border of life and death; it has
  always been since the genesis

of the altered world. And so, without qualm,
  I'll retreat to the warmth of

my autumn bed, and slumber deep just above
  the coming frost; there I'll

dream *my* fast-approaching winter dreams,
  and leave behind autumn's flux.

Uncle Delbert's Poems

If a rhyme alone could make a poem,
coupled with the knowledge of one's
place in time, then Uncle Delbert was
the Robert Frost of Pennsylvania.

Now long dead, his widow, my Great-
Aunt Verne, pulled from a roll-top desk
an envelope filled with typed poems—
each year's output fastened together
with straight pins & a certain sentiment.

Uncle Delbert did not fill his poems
with discouragement, doubt or despair,
although there was plenty to go around
with the Depression, world war, and
death. His quiet poems of season came
and went in the pages of his small town
newspaper without much critical notice,
yet cherished by those who knew how
remarkable a simple, honest life really is,
and relished the mystery of its passing.

I tucked my uncle's poems under my
arm and headed home to file them away
until the next generation of family poet
could pass on this great, abundant legacy.

Taking Stock

In the early morning light
I lay an arm across your side.
Now awake, I am an *island in
the stream*—subject to the storms
that come with the wind, and you are
a small boat tied carelessly to my shore.

Together, we are a moment of stillness,
a place of calm in a sea of change, even
as the space is growing between our
bodies as the universe expands.
Perhaps if we hold on tight,
it will be content to rest
here—just for a while.

December in the Woods

*To speak truly, few adult
persons can see nature.
—Ralph Waldo Emerson,
 from his journal*

My person sits by a stream in early
winter, in woods with no snow,
only wetness—an indifference
that's stripped the earth to a vulgar
nakedness.

In her loss of innocence…
a broken-down stone wall lies like
the weathered bones of an animal
that dreamed quietly in the final
minutes before death.

Rusted wire and rotted posts
weave through since grown trees.
Cardboard posted signs—grayed
and diminished, eventually will fall
to earth and decay, sleeping deep
in her embrace.

Yet, even in her vulnerability,
these are possessions to which
nature pays no heed, boundaries
that the earth simply ignores, claims
she does not respect.

As I sit by a stream in these winter
woods, the sound of moving water
is the only essence of nature's
consciousness—except, of course,
for my own languid thoughts,

which also spring from someplace
deep within *my* being. It would appear
that both nature and my person are
quietly searching for their source
under the watching eye of God.

Daydreaming

*In my study...A different
conception of mind evolved:
one that lets things happen
and also makes things happen...
mind as functioning along one
unbroken conscious-unconscious
continuum.*
—Harold Rugg, in "Imagination"

Some call it a waste of time—
that drifting of the mind...
the materialist's monster hiding
under the bed, the empty void
that floats just out of reach of
the infinite arm of science and
technology.
Perhaps, they think it's part of
the quantum world—full of
uncertainty and chaos...or
a brazen display of the *self*—
that mythological bugaboo that
plagues the abundance of facts &
figures pouring out of quantum
computers, or simply coming
forth from the squishy matter in
our heads. Oh yes, they say, it's
those electrical firings and
chemical reactions, those
overworked neurons that cause
us to act human at the most
inopportune times...
Like when I wonder if the world
would look different in a foreign
language, or what's it like to live
in top of a very tall tree. I'm
not alone—if we dare consider

30

other souls: The poet James
Wright daydreamed while lying
in a hammock in Minnesota,
his reflections—the rebirth of
his literary career.
No doubt Paris fantasized a lot
about Helen before boarding a
ship for Troy—two one-way
tickets in his hot, little hand.

Dr. King had a vision that
compelled him to a Birmingham
jail, a history-defining speech in
D.C., and finally a martyr's death
in Memphis—all because the
synapses fired, in a certain order,
and the chemicals flowed in
certain channels.
Some go as far as saying these
things never happened…our
memories are nothing more than
circuits misbehaving.

Call it what you will, there's
no end to such extreme,
unexamined dreaming.

Imperfection

Poem to a Grandfather I Never Knew

—for Clayton Bird (1882–1940)

O clay man, are you roaming again
the timeless bone-yards of eternity,
urgently seeking the satisfaction you
seemed never to find in earthly life?
I hear you turn over ancient stones,
rattle yellowed papers, and thud

through ruins like a hunter of lost
treasures in the fitful and aimless
sleep assigned you.
Perhaps you seek a vagrant mother,
absent in self-exile from nine sons
for weeks at a time—no note of
explanation left on the kitchen table.

Left to fend for yourself, you end up
crossing your arms in a '39 photo at
the World's Fair. Do you hide a hole
left in your chest?
And so, from lumberman to laborer,
from tenant farmer, to handyman,
you roamed until a foolish, illicit
death from a jazzed-up libido and a
failing heart.
I imagine the woman at the hospital,
where you worked, as desperate as you—
a person with no name and no future,
looking to hitch on your unreachable
dreams.

O clay man, how much you missed—
including me, whose anger blossomed
at finding you gone. Your ghost has
long haunted my lost and muted
memories. Is it right for me to mourn
our history—you and I, a history
connected only by name, blood and
time? Yet, clearly, it's the history that
beats in your grandson's heart.

A Short History of Failure

Stop trusting in man who is but a breath
in his nostrils; of what account is he?
                              —Isaiah 2:22

I.

Eve, having forgotten the facts of life,
lost her argument with the devil, while
Adam—distracted and sulking because
the serpent hadn't spoken to *him,* chose
to ignore the consequences of his pride.

He later recalled just outside the Gates
of Eden, the flaming sword still throwing
off heat after all these years:

I felt my lips and tongue
being pulled away from the inside,
resignation settled on my silence
like heavy dust. I could not respond—
even as my eyes envisioned a wilderness
stretching afar until time had no more
reign or desire.

Eve, angry and frustrated at Adam's
impotence, spent her days writing post
cards to old friends: *wish you were here.*
It's much lonelier than paradise.

II.

Adam continued his story—one eye on
the wrath of God, the other on the dust,
packed hard at his feet.

Back and forth we came, looking for
the familiar. Yet, somewhere along
the way the distance became too much,
the maps all neatly drawn on the back
of our hands had faded. It was lengths
of time like long tangled strings that
we were caught up in. For the old places
had changed. Old voices were gone,
taking with them the old truths, the old
meanings. New voices had entered, and
we no longer understand the language.
Our favorite stories—the histories of our
young lives, written out on crumbling tablets,
had been wiped away countless times.

All the while, Eve continued to scribble on
postcards—her frustration ever growing
at the lack of response she received.

III.

While his old eyes searched the dimmed
horizon for a clue, Adam recalled a moment
He experienced a long time ago.

I remember one evening…the early
spring air was exceptionally warm.
The heavens could not discern the
contradiction. Soon the confused sky
rumbled. The rain came and I knew
tomorrow would be colder. It was then
I understood: Innocence is perhaps too
heavy a memory for anyone to bear.

Eve sighed at the story and silently
returned to her correspondence—
hoping for just one more good day.

Some Thoughts in Early Winter

While I ponder what to scrawl in
my notebook, I sip lukewarm tea
and listen to the sounds of classical
music. Beyond my window, the air
has turned colder. Flurries are
falling from a metallic sky, the light
draining from the day as if the
batteries of the world are running low.

A weather report—or am I thinking
more of my aging life? Seeking a place
to take my thoughts, I open a tin with
dancing bears painted on the lid—
filled with small objects from my past.
Yes, I'm a 'keeper,' saving mementos
in various boxes, the detritus of my
days, things of no real worth—except
for what they might say to me now.

Take for instance an orange ribbon
from a bridesmaid's dress, once worn
by my future wife many years ago.
It still speaks of new love, fresh with
discovery and desire. That love is as
real today, but different: perhaps
less passionate, but deeper and more
durable, less callow and more mature,
hopefully, less caring for my own
satisfaction than I care for hers.

Did I keep this bit of orange ribbon
as a symbol of possession—tying us
together for fear of losing her love?

Now, I keep it to remember—
I must never bind myself too tightly
to the ones I love, to let them live
freely within the circle of my affection.

Oh, what thoughts in early winter, as
I sip cold tea from a nearly empty cup.

The Old Dog and the Storm

—For Tego (2004–2019)

Late summer—the warm, dense
air at midnight signals its seasonal
distress with jagged, electrical
stabs at the heart of the earth.
Open violence rips apart the night
sky in a brilliance of light, while
its trailing sound and static charge
registers with the sleeping old dog,
who, now awake, begins to pant
hard like a steam locomotive on
a steep, uphill grade. Soon…

the old dog digs at the carpet,
but elderly legs betray her; she
seeks concealment, a place to
hide from some canine dread.
With unsure eyes the old dog
surveys the room's deep shadows,
then circles like a dancer under
strobes of lightning; her partner—
a dark, incomprehensible danger
that all her primal fears and
instincts have made strong in the
weakness of her ancient and
aging brain.

With no clear sensation, she poops
mightily on the bathroom floor,
then lays near the tub in watch of
another danger, another enemy
to enter her shrinking domain.
It's a terror that befalls an old dog

in the night. Come dawn, being
tired from her burden, she will
sleep deep and dreamless til well
past noon.

The Interview

After reading
an essay
on faces
by Epstein,
A man turned
to his wife,
reading in bed
next to him,
and asked her
to describe
his features.

After a
moment's
struggle,
she said,
well…
not ordinary.
Interesting…
different!

He asked, *you*
mean like a
Picasso portrait?

She wouldn't say.

Turning
on his side,
he found
himself

wondering
if his left ear
was really
his nose.

But then he
remembered:
Picasso mostly
painted women.
He turned to
his wife again,

You mean I have
a feminine face?

She wouldn't say.

This story
could go on
from here,
but it doesn't.
Like most things
in this life
it ends without
a conclusion.

At a Harvest Poetry Reading

One year was under a leaky
trailer roof—the stuff of
outlaws or sedentary Gypsies,
oral presentations lost in the
fuss of young children and
a sore, restless bottom.

Today in light drizzle but
open air, Rhonda, the
featured poet, proclaims
her art. Typed poems grow
slack in her fingers,
lavender nails flashing back
and forth between damp
pages and her blond head—
pulling strands of mist laden
hair away from her pale face.
Attractive poets either
distract or keep you hanging
on their every word.

Her stories are from child
hood—all about loss.
I envision her past fleeing
out into the open field
around us before the poet
can make it perform another
tortured retelling of itself.
Yet, her disposition gentle,
mood both pensive and
bright, no inhibitions at
the candor of her poems,
no shame in her vulnerable
humanity—she draws back

her refugee memories with
a clear reading. Bravely,
she faces again the things
that formed her life.

Auger Falls

is a giant V cut into the moraine
of the mountainside, whose
middle is a tumble and jumble
of giant rocks wedged in like balls
in a check-valve—which doesn't
stop the cascading water, but
adds to the sound & fury of its
continuous advance, slicing its
way into a dark green pool which
rushes beyond into a narrower cut
                and out of sight.

I sit looking from the safety of a
bordering ledge of rock, tempted
but hesitant to get too near the
raging cataract for fear of being
swept down its compelling but
terrifying throat—swept down
like the strewn boulders of
millennia in a cataclysmic throw
of the dice—swept down and
forever lost to a secure passage
from an appointed beginning to
an appointed end—swept away
        into another
               conceivable me.

The List

I decided to make a list.
For a long time I put it off,
afraid of what it could
become. At first I wavered—
what would be worthy of
making a list. My triumphs?
My adventures? Perhaps
I could list all my good
character traits? You know…
those things people never
notice, yet believe they are
lying about when forced
to say something pleasing
about you.

However, on a particularly
empty day, void of color
or warmth, I decided to list
what I felt was missing in
my life. I started quite fast,
aggravations of a lifetime
lining up in columns of ink
like determined men going
off to war. Nevertheless,
when finally I ran out of
fresh insults, I felt cheated;
surely the list should be
longer. So, before putting
it aside, I put *the loss of my
imagination* at the bottom
of the list.

Canoeing on Sunfish Pond

On a rainy day in a period
of much dryness—no one
really complains. Yesterday
the water was clear;
      today it's inky black.

My wife and I glide among
white and yellow water lilies
floating in clusters like
disparate groups forming
at a party. None look our
way or listen to our talk.

We stop paddling and begin
to drift. It takes a moment
to position one's self against
fixed sightings on the shore—
to determine how far, and,
hopefully, in what direction
      we have gone.

The rain becomes real as
feathery mist gives way to
a shower—hard against our
skin. We head for shore with
me bossing, she disliking it.
Somehow, I know I've lived
this day out in some form
      many
           times
                before.

Visit to a Country Pond

I've come to this country pond
many times—without knowing
its name; perhaps it has no name.
It sits alone at the edge of a wood
without boasting much in the way

of beauty. Its hidden simplicity
offers itself as a place of solitude—
existing apart from most human
drama. Sitting on a crude, homely
bench placed at the wood line—

weathered by many seasons of rain,
snow, and sun, I look over the pond's
stillness—observing the small
movements of nature in the midst
of its watery life: A young buck

drinks greedily at the pond's edge,
his thirsty eyes momentarily blind
to my presence. A muskrat swims
from his hole in the pond's shallow
bank—surveying the neighborhood

he calls home. Fish climb just above
the water's face in pursuit of tasty
flying snacks, while dragonflies skim
the algal surfaces like helicopters
filled with traffic spotters. Possibly,

they report on schools of fish
traveling back and forth to favorite
feeding spots. I ask my environs—
what are fish to a dragonfly?
Butterflies, fluttering around me,

offer no answer; their curiosity
fades as quickly as their arousal
to check me out. Biting insects stay
longer; yet, are not interested in
philosophical chats about nature,

are not aware this is a "thinker's"
bench. Then, the sound of sports car
engines drone heavy in the humid
air of August. Ten miles away men
race around an asphalt track in

search of personal glory. Plainly,
their motorized babel is divorced
from nature. This seems almost an
invasion upon the privacy of this
place, its aim—the total possession

of the very air nature breaths. Does
this insatiable lust also demand
control of our imaginations? Perhaps,
sitting on the "thinker's" bench, my
thoughts have run wild. Yet, I know—

this pond and the surrounding wood
do not strive beyond their call
to convey intimacy between all of
                    God's creatures.

A Moment to Consider

On the radio a cello
is playing . . . something
deep, slow and sad . . .

like someone crying
in the night.

It may be my youngest
daughter trying to find
her life.

It may be her father,
afraid she won't.

Friday, 6:37 AM

Okay . . .
here's how it is.
After reading a
short history on
Robert Lowell's
later poems
while lying in bed
and drinking a cup
of coffee, I open
the window blinds.

The morning light is
subdued, hesitant—
not really gray as in
so many accounts.
Though there are
no shadows—
only dark spaces,
details are slowly
blossoming.

From across a light
slate sky, the rising
sun in the east is
kissing the face of
the western moon—
making it blush
brightly as it sits
on a tree top—
the *tree*—not the
moon—just turning
green.

I'm surprised at my
awareness of such
things—due to a
deficit of solid sleep.
My aging brain—
and the manic,
overweight woman
living above, pacing
her room all night,
each step sounding
like a small caliber
pistol firing as the
floor cracks beneath
her weight—puts me
at odds with the
coming day.

But I'll manage
somehow. Don't
let it bother you.
Feel concern,
instead, for the
woman upstairs,
whose sense of
the morning
must amount to
something like
a blur.

Playing Catch with Sarah

She didn't throw like a girl . . .
the baseball hit my glove
like a projectile shot from a
cannon. My hand momentarily
stinging, I acted tough like a father
should when his daughter sends
the white sphere faster than
expected through the molecules
that make up the air on a sunny
afternoon—causing vibrations
halfway around the world.

Halfway around the world . . .
today, she's not *that* far away—
only 2/3 rd's of a continent.
I can't expect her to throw a ball
2000 miles, but I wait to receive
a phone call, maybe a text—
beckoning for comfort in her pain,
her emptiness. The sting of reception
is the same, and I, again, must be
tough like a father whose daughter's
pathos hits hard against his not so
padded emotions. So I wait,
readying myself to return my
promotion of hope, my prayers,
my love. Again, I'm throwing
a sphere back and forth with
my youngest daughter;
she—despite the expanded distance
between us–is still playing catch
with her dad.

Shop Talk

When I was a young man . . .
all my old friends spoke of muscle cars
as if they were bawdy women waiting
to be had in the back seat. Voices
quivered with anticipation for that
moment of reckless passion.

O Mother Machines! How their mouths
gargled such sweet obscenities! How they
throbbed underneath thin-skinned fingers,
tin flesh vibrating on a bed of leaf springs,
the blast of exhaust—an orgasm of extension!

Alas . . . I sat listening all night to their
stories of conquest with my ignition key
in my back pocket. My lady was a crone
gone sour with bashed in teeth, and slow
                              motion mobility.
And try as I did, there was no making
myself believe she wasn't over the hill.

Earth, Wind, Water, and Fire

My friend sits on a block of wood
across from me, talking through
feelings of betrayal, like a man
stumbling through underbrush.

Around us lay the sawed lengths
of logs ready for splitting. Some
time next winter they'll become
someone's heat, welcomed, not

like the fire that burns in his soul.
It is an anger that refuses to die,
for his wound resists any balm as
disappointment fans the embers

at the bottom of his memory.
A wind comes up, a hint of rain.
Cold now in a T-shirt, he dives into
flannel. Suddenly, words could

easily get lost in the short distance
between us. We sit – two men on
blocks of wood, each with our own
weaknesses holding us fast to the

earth, knowing we'll always struggle
to become what we want to be.
As if on cue, we walk down to a
nearby creek, running swift and

strong after last night's storm, its
current like a seductive madness.
A man could drown fast, I think,
sucked under before he knew it.

Turning, I want to say, *forgive.*
Churning water mocks my concern.
And so, I leave him to split sawed
logs in a light rain, his well-placed

blows cutting each into equal lengths.
A fire awaits their unrehearsed
                        consummation.

Instructions at the End of the World

I notice how the winter days
are bleak; seemingly, the earth
no longer sustains life. Be careful,
your faith may not be strong enough.
You should learn to walk circumspectly.

Come, walk with me in the dormant fields;
the tall, yellow grass is dry and hollow,
and have become the breathing tubes
                        of the dead.
You might be fooled into thinking
it is the wind you hear, and not
the sound of watchful sleep.
Listen carefully. Here you
will find the truth.

In the doing, if weariness draws across
your legs, striking fragile bones
like a hammer, know the world
has frozen into an angry fist.
Ignore its lack of subtlety.
It is acting out its rage.

When the winter sky throws
a hard light against your eyes,
and you are blinded by its hypocrisy,
remember, the weakened sun is in denial.
Do not try to reason away its pain.

If the hawk keeps circling above, his eye
searching for the slightest motion,
he is looking to survive beyond
the passing of time and space.
You must understand this as
a sign: Our reward is not
always in the here
and now.

You may feel uncertain. *Hold on*
to your love for as long as you can.
For in the waiting, a particularly
lonely night will open its empty
arms, and your hopes will dance
under the cold, ecstatic moonlight,

her bone-white legs dangling as if
on strings. Even in a threadbare,
house-dress dream, her heart will beat
in perfect rhythm to the music coming
                                  from above.

About the Author

T.P. Bird is a retired industrial drafter/designer and minister. He has been reading and writing poetry since being in the Army at Ft. Ord near Monterey, CA in 1969. He found a collection of Leonard Cohen's poetry on Fisherman's Wharf and went on from there. He has published in *Relief Quarterly, Penwood Review, BoomerLit, Poetry Quarterly, Common Ground Review, Miller's Pond, Tiny Seed Literary Journal,* and a chapbook, *Scenes and Speculations* (Finishing Line Press). He and his wife live in Lexington, KY.